M000316891

Be You
by Design

The Ultimate Guide in Discovering You Through Design

BY GERALDINE HOWE

DORRANCE
PUBLISHING CO
EST. 1920
PITTSBURGH, PENNSYLVANIA 15238

The contents of this work, including, but not limited to, the accuracy of events, people, and places depicted; opinions expressed; permission to use previously published materials included; and any advice given or actions advocated are solely the responsibility of the author, who assumes all liability for said work and indemnifies the publisher against any claims stemming from publication of the work.

All Rights Reserved
Copyright © 2021 by Geraldine Howe

No part of this book may be reproduced or transmitted, downloaded, distributed, reverse engineered, or stored in or introduced into any information storage and retrieval system, in any form or by any means, including photocopying and recording, whether electronic or mechanical, now known or hereinafter invented without permission in writing from the publisher.

Dorrance Publishing Co
585 Alpha Drive
Suite 103
Pittsburgh, PA 15238
Visit our website at *www.dorrancebookstore.com*

ISBN: 978-1-6480-4281-2
eISBN: 978-1-6480-4876-0

Be You by Design

The Ultimate Guide in Discovering You Through Design

THIS BOOK IS DEDICATED TO

the memory of Dr. Robert Whiteside,
who helped guide me through my own journey of self-discovery.

Table of Contents

Acknowledgments

Completion of this book came about through the encouragement and support of my family and friends. My gratitude and appreciation go to Ginny Flynn, who gave me unlimited support and helped shape this book from the beginning. I would also like to think Cat Saunders for her professional editing directions, which were invaluable in writing this book.

I am grateful to Natasha Downing, my former teacher, who continues to light the path before me. Thanks also to Elena Christensen's wonderful persistence and hard work in helping to construct the contents of this book.

Last but not least, I want to thank my four wonderful children—Diane, Monique, Marc, and Eric—and Sophia Lowe Hines, who have been incredibly supportive of my work with *Be You by Design*.

Foreword

Since we are not clones but each of us has different tastes, the key to interior decorating is *individualizing*. Have things the way *you* want them. That always suits you. (Or if you use a professional interior decorator, the way your client wants its.)

Much of our traits and preferences are built in by nature. If you have more than one child, you already know how different native dispositions can be. Except, of course, for identical twins. An example: Identical twin girls, separated at birth and raised apart, one in England and the other in Australia, found when they were grown and met that they had each chosen the same pattern of wallpapers in decorating their homes!

Naturally, our inborn dispositions are shown somewhat in our body, especially in our face, hair, and hands.

Gerri Howe, a gifted and successful West Coast designer and decorator, has in this book added the extra dimension of *individualizing* according to the unique native liking of each person concerned—whether dramatic or aesthetic, rugged or refined, conventional or unconventional, etc. Even your child's room can be decorated to suit and delight that particular girl's or boy's nature.

Gerri Howe also shares with you key Personology traits (applied behavioral genetic traits) and how to recognize them and apply them.

Read, apply, and enjoy!

Robert L. Whiteside (deceased) President, Personology Institute
Author of the nonfiction best seller, *Face Language*

Introduction

How many times have you approached a decorating project and doubted your ability to create something that was truly a reflection of your specific needs as an individual? Perhaps the only solution you could imagine required a large budget to support the big picture. Have you ever stopped to think that the solution might be found within your own personality traits?

Personality traits can provide you with definite guidelines for design projects, and they can also offer an enlightening path of self-discovery. To a great extent, your daily life expresses many facets of your individual personality traits. Such traits can give you tangible information about yourself, which in turn can help you create a visual picture that represents your specific needs as an individual.

Each of your personality traits can be used as a clue. If you can imagine all of these clues coming together like puzzle pieces, you will have discovered some important elements that can help you create a quality design that no amount of money can guarantee. By utilizing your individual personality traits, you can expect results that truly express your personal style. This should be the ultimate goal in any personal decorating project, whether it is for your work or home environment.

Be You by Design can help you eliminate the doubt and worry so often connected with decorating projects. It can also help you transform your decorating experience into a creative and fulfilling adventure. With the support of this book, you can design the kind of solid structure that assures decorating excellence on all levels.

You may be surprised at how much easier decorating can be if you utilize your personality traits as significant guidelines and principles. These traits can enable you to approach your decorating projects with a higher degree of awareness. This awareness can assist you in activating all of your creative talents, even those that have been lying dormant. Above all, with the support of this book, you can invite creativity into the fabric of your daily life, bringing more originality, playfulness, and excitement to everything around you.

Chapter One
Decorating – An Expression of Personality Style

People express their unique individuality through many facets of life. The extent of your own creativity will determine how much of your true self is expressed in daily life. Two of the most obvious and familiar forms of personal expression can be seen in the way people decorate their homes or choose clothing for their wardrobes.

You have probably met people who are good examples of clearly expressed personal style. When you walk down the street or through the local shopping mall, you may spot a flamboyant hat worn by a woman, or a colorful shirt or necktie worn by a businessman. The hat may represent the **Dramatic Trait**, while the colorful shirt or necktie may be a reflection of the **Aesthetic Trait**. These are only two of the many personality traits that provide specific information about the qualities that make us different from one another.

Decorating involves a process that also includes the expression of personal style. This process can be made easier if you understand the relationship between specific personality traits and various decorating styles. To get you started in thinking about this relationship between personality traits and decorating styles, you can try the following exercise.

First, take out a piece of paper and make a quick list of the personality traits that best describe you. Just use whatever words feel right for you. If you notice that several traits seem related, feel free to group those traits together under one general category.

Next, write each trait or category at the top of a separate piece of paper. Underneath each personality trait, place photographs or magazine pictures which represent that particular trait to you. By doing this simple project, you can begin to discover important clues that you can use for your creative ventures, including the decoration of your personal space.

If you are willing to explore who you are through your personality traits, then decorating your home or office environment can become your original work of art. By working with your personality traits, you can get a good visual picture of your personal style. In this way, decorating helps you create an original portrait of your uniqueness.

Everyone has the opportunity to live happy and abundant lives. Within each of us lies the power to create each day through self-discovery and self-awareness, and this same power acts as a catalyst to move you toward a process of inner growth that can last a lifetime. You can nurture this process in all your experiences by exploring and learning about who you are. This is a journey that has no end.

My own life moved to a new level of awareness when I discovered Personology, which is the study of the relationship between human structure and behavior. Personology helped me discover some of my true gifts, talents, and abilities, and it helped me understand some of the traits that I could strengthen in order to better utilize these gifts and abilities.

Personology has made my process of self-discovery a joyful and enlightening one. It has given me a clear vision of the power and magnificence I possess—the same power and magnificence that exists within you as well. If you choose to share this journey with me, you, too, may clarify your vision of a life filled with creativity and productivity.

With every venture comes the opportunity to tap into your creative self and follow the true path of self-discovery and personal awareness. Contained within the core of your being is a giant force waiting to be acknowledged. Once this power is released, you can rise to a new level of excellence as your life takes on new meaning and purpose.

Your uniqueness and individuality holds the key that unlocks the door to this power— the power of your own creativity. Creativity, in turn, always has a traveling companion: magic. Magic is an element of life that is often overlooked or regarded as unimportant. People may even believe that it exists only in the imagination or not at all. However, whenever you activate your creative juices, magic always follows!

By discovering your inherent personality traits—and decorating according to them— you can bring more magic into your home or office environment. In this way, decorating can contribute an abundance of fun and practical knowledge, and it can give you a foundation for ongoing creativity in every aspect of your daily life.

Chapter Two
Introduction to Personology

THE SCIENCE OF GENETICS

Personology is a way of understanding individual human structure (inherent genetic traits) and their relationship to behavior. To the degree that you understand and utilize your inherent traits, you can realize your individual powers and accomplish your personal goals.

Trait factors are *inclinations*, and personal behavior is established through trait interaction, not through any single trait. No trait operates in a vacuum. In addition, choice always supersedes structure, which basically means that free will can override the natural inclinations indicated by a particular person's genetic structure.

BASIC PREMISES

Human structure is inherent, and it predisposes individuals toward specific kinds of expression and response. This inherent structure indicates your basic disposition, native inclinations of function, and personal limitations. However, external circumstances may modify or limit your natural style of expression or response. The lasting effect of any experience is determined by the person receiving and recording that experience, not by the experience itself. Therefore, individual consciousness is more powerful than circumstances.

STRUCTURE/FUNCTION AND PERSONALITY

Robert Whiteside, former President of Interstate College of Personology in Capistrano, California, wrote:

> *Aristotle, the father of science, selected his pupils (including the youth who later developed into Alexander the Great) from their structure. Aristotle said a full-fledged science should be developed from the study of the connection between an individual's unique build and his unique capacities.*

Personology is this science. It is built on 20th century methodology with complete statistical validation. In this background are the principles of the relationship between structure and function. The foreground is the detailed daily life technique of Personology, pinpointing for the individual how to best direct daily life to increase happiness and effectiveness.

Two general premises apply:

1. Structure inclines toward corresponding function (human anatomy relates to human function); and
2. Choice supersedes structure (the human nervous system is built so that each person can consciously make choices about direction).

Dan Whiteside, Director of Structure/Function Research for the Interstate College of Personology in Capistrano, California, is credited for emphasizing that structure/function principles are a modern, logical, nonstandard explanation as to why Personology techniques work so well in understanding individual daily activities.

Traits are neither good nor bad in themselves. They are rather advantageous—or not— in relation to the ways people express them. For example, the trait of **high tolerance** is not "good" per se, and **low tolerance** is not necessarily "bad."

By consciously directing himself, a person who is highly tolerant can retain the advantages of broad planning and a philosophical approach to life without incurring the disadvantages of procrastination and sloppiness that might otherwise result from being overly tolerant. On the other hand, a low-tolerance person can keep the advantages of dependability and precision workmanship, without experiencing the disadvantages of pettiness or narrow-mindedness that could arise from examining things too closely.

Thus, the structure/function concept clarifies that highly tolerant people are simply broader in their vision and not necessarily messy unless they allow themselves to be. Similarly, low-tolerance people are not "intolerant" unless they allow themselves to go that direction.

Thus, the inner intent is the same for people of both polarities. Understanding this, high-tolerance people cannot be accused of purposefully forgetting to take care of things before they get out of hand, and low-tolerance people cannot be accused of trying to control everything. On the inside, each person intends to do a proper job. There is simply a high need to express personal traits through specific behavioral styles, and Personology techniques can help you understand the best way to do this.

OTHER SCIENCES BACK STRUCTURE/FUNCTION AND PERSONOLOGY

At the same time the broader picture of principle-and-application has been presented by the Interstate College of Personology and its structure/function department, companion sciences have been developing explosively. The development of these companion sciences—from DNA research to the laser beam—has backed up Personology.

The invention of the electron microscope, which enlarges in the proportion of making a 25-cent piece look as big as Central Park, has unlocked the genetic code and made DNA and RNA common terms. It is now easy to understand that your eye color and many other things about your individual makeup—such as your athletic or musical ability—have something to do with your physical structure.

Perhaps the most incisive finding in recent years (of a companion science that backs up Personology) comes from James Shields, an English scientist. With the help of the British Broadcasting Company, Dr. Shields gathered together data concerning 44 pairs of identical twins who had been raised in different homes. He compared them with 44 sets of twins raised in the same household.

In an article called "Twins Brought Up Apart" in *Eugenics-Review* (1958), Dr. Shields wrote:

> *Identical twins who had seldom, or never, met before the study, proved much more alike in PERSONALITY, INTELLIGENCE, TEMPERAMENT, ATTITUDES, and MANNERISMS than are fraternal twins brought up in the same household.*

American and British biologists have begun to stress that, with the approach of the possibility of change, human genes can influence heredity. Humans have decisions to make just as important for the future of mankind as what to do with the atomic bomb. Should a race be raised, they ask, with more brains than brawn?

The spirit of the times has caught up with Personology and is favorable to it. However, other techniques have not yet caught up with Personology in terms of its counseling techniques, practical applications, or its all-encompassing philosophy. Personology is a timely interdisciplinary science that combines physical sciences (such as biology) with the study of human psychology and function.

Personology is a methodology. It is a technique for recognizing specific functions related to specific human structure. Its aim is to enhance self-direction for the individual through understanding his or her structure/function relationship. Thus, effective "self-government" is its primary goal.

The unique contribution of Personology in the field of human understanding is its approach to counseling people in regard to individual differences. The emphasis of this approach is to encourage the individuality of each person through conscious self-control.

FIVE BASIC AREAS OF TRAITS

There are five basic areas of traits as described by Personology:

1. **The Physical Traits** - These are traits of basic physical structure and current physical condition. Of these traits, the most important is **Physical Insulation**.

2. **The Automatic Expression Traits** - These are mechanisms of expression. They are not conscious functions. They are automatic in their operation. Because of this, they are the most important traits over which to gain control in the moment. Of these, the most important traits are **Impetuousness, Instinctive Self-Reliance**, and **Automatic Resistance**.

3. **The Feeling/Emotion Traits** - These traits form the inherent motivations and conscious feelings and reactions of the individual. They are the most important traits in Personology. Of these traits, **Innate Self-Confidence, Balance**, and **Tolerance** are the most important. These traits form the basic perception (**Tolerance**), reception of experience (**Innate Self-Confidence**), and record of experience (**Balance**).

4. **The Action Traits** - These traits indicate the action potential of the individual. The most important are **Progressiveness** and **Forcefulness**. **Progressiveness** indicates a person's long-range action potential. **Forcefulness** represents the individual's force of action in the moment.

5. **The Thinking Traits** – These traits indicate the thinking potential of the individual. Quality of thought, however, is determined by the *use* of cells, not by the *quantity* of cells. The most important traits in this area are **Multiplicity of Ideas, Thinking, Resoluteness**, and **Imaginativeness**.

In this book, 12 basic personality traits will be described in further detail, and their relationship with decorating choices will be shown through case studies and photographic examples. Without a doubt, you will recognize yourself in some of these traits, and you will see how to use these traits to your advantage in home and office design.

Chapter Three
Personality Traits

The 12 personality traits that will be described here are: Dramatic, Adventurousness, Aesthetic, Imaginativeness, Conservation, Construction, High Physical Insulation, Low Physical Insulation, Backward Balance, Forward Balance, Idealizing, and Practical. Each of these particular traits can be recognized through facial characteristics. Hopefully, you will enjoy identifying some of these traits in friends, family, and yourself by reviewing the illustrations included with this chapter.

TRAIT: DRAMATIC

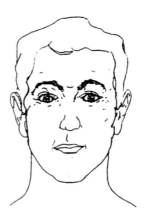

Figure 3-1
Characteristic: High, sweeping, arched eyebrows

According to Personology, high, sweeping, arched eyebrows represent the **Dramatic** trait (figure 3.1). If you possess this trait, you may have a true gift for make-believe. You can get into the spirit of a situation. Most likely, you may also find it easy to fit into any role. The dramatic person loves to make sweeping entrances and exits. Drama and spirit enliven everything they do.

Decorating with this trait requires dramatic touches to reflect the personal flair for flamboyance. This kind of person is attracted to any underlying theme that says, "Look at me, this is who I am!"

Perhaps you have visited a home that projected this dramatic flair through the use of furniture or other objects that were entirely different from anything you had ever seen. In other cases, people with this trait may pick out one focal point and decorate around that. Either way, this kind of room design can have a powerful effect on anyone who enters the space.

The person with the **Dramatic** trait may also like to have a number of items that stand out and grab your attention. Some examples of this would be an art print on the wall with an unusual color combination, or a rug that depicts a pattern that stimulates your visual attention. Anything that is eye-catching will feel dramatic to most people. Furniture in unusual places and brilliant colors that say "hello" when you enter the room—these are just a few examples of the ways a dramatic person may decorate.

TRAIT: ADVENTUROUSNESS

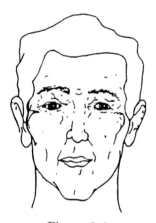

Figure 3-2
Characteristic: High, prominent cheekbones

What do the faces of American Indians, Mongols, and Vikings often have in common? They all have high, prominent cheekbones, which are characteristic of the **Adventurousness** trait (figure 3.2). If you have this trait, your biggest adventure in life will be your own self-unfoldment.

Decorating for you may include a wonderful potpourri of styles, colors, and motifs. Anything goes because you are open to all kinds of ideas. A mixture of things—such as different periods of furniture—will be par for the course. It's not likely that you will be satisfied with common trends, because that would only limit the abundance of ideas you already have brewing in your own mind.

People with the trait of **Adventurousness** may want to make changes in their decorating scheme quite often. If you are this kind of person, you may like to change colors, add another accessory, or change the furniture arrangement more often than most. It may help you to work with neutral colors, because they can provide you with a background for frequent color changes in your accent furniture or accessory objects. In addition, pictures or mementos from your travels can also add spice to your decorating theme.

TRAIT: AESTHETIC

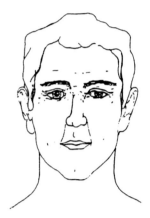

Figure 3-3
Characteristic: Flat, straight eyebrows

The physical indicator for the **Aesthetic** trait (figure 3.3) is flat, straight eyebrows. People with this trait tend to make an art out of any project or situation, and they often end up in a profession that involves art, music, or literature. This trait represents those who are artists at heart.

If you reflect this trait, you may have a strong need to make your decorating project an extremely creative one. It may also be especially meaningful for you to listen to your favorite music while arranging your furniture! Dining by candlelight could be another source of enjoyment for you. Surrounding yourself with harmony is of prime importance.

For those who possess the **Aesthetic** trait, it will be essential for you to express your favorite kind of art as a feature ingredient in your decorating. Color is also essential for you. Restful hues such as green and blue tones, neutral tones, and pastels can support you, because these represent soothing colors for you. Of course, each of these components must come together harmoniously in whatever space you are decorating.

TRAIT: IMAGINATIVENESS

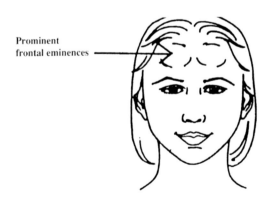

Prominent
frontal eminences

Figure 3-4
Characteristic: Prominent frontal eminences

The essence of the trait of **Imaginativeness** trait (figure 3.4) is the power to form mental images or concepts for that which is not present to the physical senses. This trait also carries a connotation of a free-thinking, creative mind that can visualize qualities or happenings.

Imaginativeness is in the thinking traits area. Semantically, the word "imaginativeness" is used in Personology since the word "imagination" is sometimes associated with daydreaming. On the other hand, **Imaginativeness** conveys a sense of power to visualize freely without straying too far into the world of unreality. Naturally, there will be variations among individuals, depending on the other traits that influence someone's outer expression.

For you, what makes a room *come alive* in your imagination? If you possess the **Imaginativeness** trait, you may find it easy to visualize your decorating project entirely in your head. With this gift of imagination, your capacity to come up with great ideas will be limitless. You are probably the kind of person who can have fun with innovative ideas that may not be found in most magazines or decorating books.

Accessories may be a main focus for you, because they can play an important role in pulling a project together. For you, accessories will be like spice in food. You may be attracted to unusual items, such as colorful objects, conversation pieces, or decorative accents that evoke strong responses because of their uniqueness.

Creatively bound books, artwork from specific cultures, or vases with different textures may all appeal to you. Area rugs that display patterns in colors you love can bring excitement to your space. Dried flowers, interesting lighting, and carefully selected designs can also accentuate your **Imaginativeness** trait.

A tip for someone with this trait is to have pictures in a scrapbook that show furnishings and accessories you like—just to stimulate your own imagination. Once you have photographic examples, you can use them to help you visualize the kind of space that would most suit you personally. If you have the trait of **Imaginativeness**, be sure to take plenty of time to enjoy the process of decorating creatively. Let your imagination flow!

TRAITS: CONSERVATION AND CONSTRUCTION

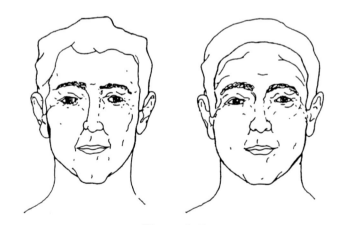

Figure 3-5
Basic Body Types: Ectomorphs, Endomorphs, and Mesomorphs

Before outlining the **Conservation** and **Construction** traits (figures 3.5) and their decorating tips, it may be helpful to mention the three basic groups of human structure as originally described by Robert L. Whiteside in his book, *Face Language*. Generally speaking, people fall into one of three main categories of physical structure: ectomorphs, endomorphs, and mesomorphs.

Ectomorphs have triangular-shaped faces, with a large crown (top of the head). They have a comparatively high proportion of ectoderm (nervous tissue), and they are more thinking-oriented than the other groups. Ectomorphs will usually respond to experiences from a mental, rather than physical, perspective.

Endomorphs have roundish faces and bodies, and they have a large proportion of endoderm (digestive tissue) compared to other people. These people are big on food, entertainment, and physical comfort. They are natural hosts, cooks, and politicians. Endomorphs are typically gregarious and jovial, and they like to put down roots. They savor everything sensual, including lovemaking. People with this body structure hate to see anything go to waste, and therefore, these are the people who exhibit the **Conservation** trait.

Of the three body types, mesomorphs have the most muscular build, with a squarish overall shape and a relatively high proportion of mesoderm (the middle of the three primary germ layers of the embryo that develops into the skeletal and muscular systems). These are the people who build, dig, and change the face of the earth. They are generally career-minded, as opposed to being homemakers. Thus, mesomorphs would be good examples of people with the Construction trait.

TRAIT: CONSERVATION

Characteristic: A round-shaped forehead

The **Conservation** trait is found in the round-faced person. These kinds of people enjoy talking about their homes. In addition, they are usually very fond of food, and they seem to know where all the best restaurants are located. Entertaining at home is also important to people with this trait.

If you possess the trait of **Conservation**, you may want to design a home environment that will accommodate your flair for entertaining and your penchant for comfort. Those who fall into this group will usually prefer large kitchens with all the latest appliances, and they may create room arrangements that cater to sensual pleasure and physical ease.

Conservation individuals may find themselves hosting parties that feature elegant china and silverware, fresh flowers, and a sprinkling of candles to light the night. Warm colors are typically favored by people with this trait, and those of you who fit this description may find that home decorating is pure joy for you.

TRAIT: CONSTRUCTION

Characteristic: A broad forehead, with square-shaped face

As mentioned earlier in the section about the three body types, **Construction** individuals are mesomorphs—those with squarish faces and muscular builds. These people are likely to put their career first, and they will probably not spend much time at home. Such people do not usually give much time or attention to rest or food. Instead, they like to talk about their career plans or other worldly activities.

Women as well as men can exhibit this trait. As much as these people love their families, they may feel as if their feet are set in cement if they find themselves trapped in mundane domestic routines.

If you are someone with the **Construction** trait, you would probably benefit from a home office specifically decorated according to your personal tastes. Since work is of prime importance to you, you may need a space a home that supports your career activities. You might want to include bulletin boards, bookcases, and computer systems, along with personal accents and good-sized plants.

TRAIT: PHYSICAL INSULATION

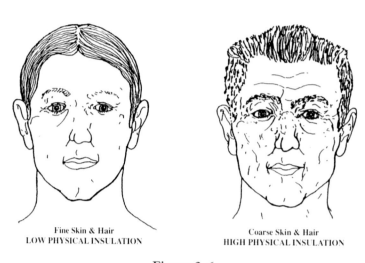

Fine Skin & Hair
LOW PHYSICAL INSULATION

Coarse Skin & Hair
HIGH PHYSICAL INSULATION

Figure 3-6
Definition: Basic timing of nerve response
Range of characteristics: Fine skin and hair Medium-textured skin and hair; Coarse skin and hair

The trait of **Physical Insulation** traits (figures 3.6) is particularly noticeable in hair texture. You—or someone you know—may have "baby hair" that is almost like silken fiber. Fine hair like this is a good indication of the **Low Physical Insulation** trait. People with this trait are often referred to as being thin-skinned, because they are usually more sensitive, both physically and emotionally. On the opposite side of the continuum are those with coarse skin and hair, which indicates **High Physical Insulation.**

In general, the **Physical Insulation** trait measures a person's innate sensitivity to external circumstances. That is, it measures a person's physical timing of reception. The more insulation a person has, the more stimuli it takes to "reach through" to his or her awareness. Conversely, those with less insulation will require less stimulation to experience the same effect.

The thicker the first layer of skin, the longer and stronger a stimulus must be to get through to a person's nerve receptors. The thinner the first layer of skin, the quicker the stimulus will reach the nerve receptors. Since it takes longer for anything to affect a person with **High Physical Insulation,** such a person will usually be slower to react. The reverse is true for a person with thin skin or **Low Physical Insulation.**

People with medium-textured skin and hair do not have the sensitivity of the finer— nor the vigor of the coarser—extremes. They function more easily in life because they are able to give and take with more balance in their physical circumstances and personal relationships. Their only problem comes in dealing with one extreme or the other. To the fine-textured individual, the middle-range person seems coarse; to the coarse-textured individual, the middle-range person seems too sensitive. It is simply a matter of degree. If the middle-range person remains aware of this, he or she can relate compassionately with either extreme.

DECORATING TIPS FOR PHYSICAL INSULATION TRAITS

Pastel and neutral colors would be good choices for those with **Low Physical Insulation**. If you have this trait, rough fabrics will not appeal to you as much as finely textured ones, such as silk, satin, and organdy. In addition, it will be essential for you to let your feelings guide you toward colors, comfort, and styles that support your heightened level of sensitivity.

People with **High Physical Insulation** have a strong tendency to want and need more of everything. If you have this trait, you are likely to have a more rugged demeanor about you. This trait exemplifies a love of the outdoors and a preference for larger amounts of food than most people want. In addition, you may be quite comfortable with different extremes of temperature.

What do these preferences mean when you are assessing needs for decorating? No doubt you will be drawn to textured fabrics and vibrant colors. No pastels for you! Furniture that is massive can work well for you, so forget about anything that falls in the category of dainty. Dark, rich woods, such as mahogany and rosewoods, can make a strong statement for you. A few pieces of sculpted furniture can add interest. Above all, furniture should be sturdy and comfortable.

One time, I remember preparing a decorating proposal for a couple. The husband was **High Physical Insulation**, and the wife was **Low Physical Insulation**: direct opposites. When I asked them to tell me about the things they like most in their surroundings, they each had a different vision. The husband wanted strong, vibrant colors, such as burgundy, hunter green, and rich, dark browns. His wife loved neutral, lighter colors.

I knew that it would be easy to create a visual picture that would be satisfying to both of them. Through pictures, fabric swatches, and paint chips, I showed them how a combination of both their traits could be addressed. I recommended rustic, heavy, dark wood furniture and window treatments that allowed the outside view to be brought indoors. The lighter colors created a welcoming backdrop, while the darker woods presented a well-balanced and harmonious effect. The husband and wife were happy to see both of their visions represented, without one or the other dominating the room.

TRAIT: BALANCE

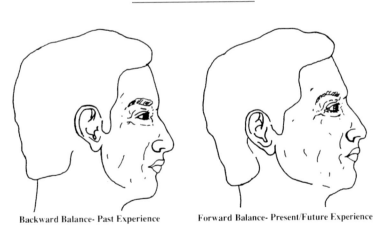

Backward Balance- Past Experience   Forward Balance- Present/Future Experience

Figure 3-8
TRAITS: FORWARD OR BACKWARD BALANCE
Characteristic: Position of the ear relative to the front or back of the head

This trait is shown by the position of the ear relative to the front or back of the head. **Forward Balance** (figure 3.8) people have more head in front of their ears than behind them (when viewed from the side). In other words, for **Forward Balance** people, their ears are positioned further back from the face.

Backward Balance (figure 3.8) people are just the opposite, with more head behind the ears than in front of them. That is, **Backward Balance** people have ears that are positioned closer to the face. Either way, this physical characteristic relates to the degree of personal need for attention, recognition, and applause.

Forward Balance people tend to think in terms of the now and the future. They thrive on immediate recognition and applause from whatever "audience" is available in the moment. People with this trait are as concerned about the future as they are about the present. These individuals work hard and exhibit a great deal of showmanship. They like to be "on stage" where everyone will notice them. Next time you watch television or a movie, notice how many of the actors have this trait!

Forward Balance people crave the spotlight and need a lot of appreciation. On the flip side, they are easily hurt by criticism. Since they are so focused on attention, they are likely to be overly concerned with the potential degree of recognition in every task, as well as the best timing for it. After all, their goal is to receive as much acknowledgment as possible for everything they do.

On the other end of the spectrum are people with the **Backward Balance** trait. These people think in terms of tradition, past experience, and positive accomplishment. They rely on past accomplishments to speak for them. They seek recognition, too, but they seek it for past accomplishments, as opposed to seeking it for the sake of personal glory.

Backward Balance people are usually more aware of the needs of others. This consideration of other people can sometimes go to the extreme of them hiding their light under the proverbial bushel. Their love of the past means they often have excellent memories, which means they don't forget things. In some ways, this can be a plus, but it may also mean that they don't forgive easily.

Because **Backward Balance** people like to compare past experiences with the present situation, their timing may be slower in the moment. On the other hand, this slower timing can help them be more poised and less anxious. People with **Backward Balance** lack showmanship, live in the past, and won't put themselves forward in an attempt to gain recognition. Their need for attention is small in comparison to the **Forward Balance** person.

DECORATING TIPS FOR FORWARD BALANCE TRAIT

If you have the trait of Forward Balance, new and trendy ideas will probably be fun for you. An unusual decor may be especially pleasing to you, and you may enjoy a decorating plan that brings you special attention.

Start with bright colors for the background—colors that inspire and excite you. You may want a home that you can show off to guests on a tour, eliciting "oohs" and "aahs" as they proceed through the various rooms. Select accessories that are unique, which can serve as conversation pieces. While it is important to have one item in each room as the main focus, a mixture of styles can also achieve an interesting look. Whatever choices you make, *style* is of great importance to you.

Entertaining can provide a ready-made audience to applaud your table settings, china, and room furnishings. You may prefer painted walls to wallpapered ones, and some walls could even be mirrored for effect. Finally, exquisite lighting can be used creatively to make your home a showcase.

DECORATING TIPS FOR BACKWARD BALANCE TRAIT

If you possess the trait of **Backward Balance**, you will certainly enjoy decorating according to a more traditional theme. Antiques will probably play a significant role, and printed fabrics such as plaids, paisleys, and floral prints may also be particularly appealing to you.

Since tradition has special meaning for those with **Backward Balance**, you may want to find objects for your space that have aged finishes or heirloom value. Examples include furniture with antique finishes or furniture that you have inherited from older family members. Small objects that represent memories from the past can also be used to complement your antique furnishings.

If you possess the trait of **Backward Balance**, you may gravitate toward dark, rich color tones. Gold tones with plaid accents may serve as a starting point, using other colors taken from the fabric itself as secondary colors. Whatever direction you go with your color scheme, choices that emphasize tradition are sure to please anyone with the trait of **Backward Balance**.

TRAIT: IDEALIZING

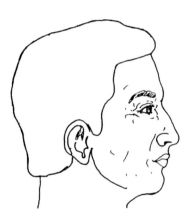

Figure 3-9
Characteristic: Low placement of the ears

For this trait, there is a relatively large percentage of the head above the ear compared to most people. The ear might even be as low as the nose opening. Another way to look at this would be to see the ear as sitting close to the collar line. This indicates the trait of **Idealizing** (figure 3.9).

Idealizing is one of my own personality traits, and it stimulates a lot of fun for me in my personal decorating projects. **Idealizing** provides an abundance of creativity. If you share this trait, you may enjoy a more lighthearted approach in your decorating scheme, with styles that include Shabby Chic and a romantic look.

Soft floral prints, checks, stripes, French antiques, and jewel tones exemplify the wide range of choices that could support someone with the trait of **Idealizing**. Lampshades with beads can also be fun, and you could add a touch of whimsy with accessories to create your own eclectic decor. In addition, those with the **Idealizing** trait might be happier with furniture and decorating accents not seen anywhere else.

TRAIT: PRACTICAL

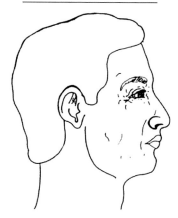

Figure 3-10
Characteristic: High placement of the ears

A person who is more practical and less idealistic will typically have ears that are positioned higher on the head. This person is more down-to-earth, less of a romantic, and less wrapped up in a principle or a cause. He or she is more willing to take whatever comes with the territory.

If you have the **Practical** trait (figure 3.10), a decorating plan for you could well include some items of furniture from the past, or so-called "traditional" items. You may enjoy purchasing antiques for your home, such as a potbelly stove for the kitchen. Family heirlooms can also add to your decorating plan.

Medium to dark colors may have special significance for you, and you might like to mix printed fabrics with familiar items you have kept through the years. Rich colors with vibrant patterns may intrigue you, and solid, sturdy wood furniture can offer balance. Pictorial magazines that focus on traditional styles of decor can give you lots of ideas to get your imagination going full speed.

Surround yourself with things that remind you of happy memories of the past. Trendy pieces of furniture are not likely to satisfy you. Consider using pictures of family members, accented by gold frames. A grouping of these might be very pleasing to you.

Wallpaper may appeal to you more than painted walls. Traditional wallpaper prints in colors such as Kelly green, gold, or wine might be good choices for you. It may help to start with three colors for your decorating plan. Rooms with lots of physical activity, such as living rooms, family rooms, and kitchens could have darker colors. Rooms that are used primarily for relaxation and recuperation, such as bedrooms or bathrooms, can use lighter colors.

Chapter Four
Introducing Color to Your Decorating

LETTING COLOR PRODUCE MAGICAL EFFECTS

Color in the environment is as necessary to personal well-being as food, water, and air. Yet for many, this element of design is given minimal attention. To introduce you to the important role of color, let me suggest a quick meditative exercise that will take just a few seconds.

To do it, simply close your eyes and imagine the room of your dreams in black and white. This may not be easy, because 80 percent of all messages related to the brain are in color. If you give it a try, I bet you'll see my point right away. Wouldn't it be a drab world without the wonder of color?

One of nature's glories is the change of seasons with all the variations of color that brings. In the fall, dark and earthy colors prevail. In the spring, lighter and brighter colors take precedence, and in the summer, pale colors dominate in nature. You can let this information about color and its relationship to the seasons help you when making seasonal changes in your home environment.

Colors were put here for a purpose. For one thing, certain colors seem to act as healing agents to the human nervous system, helping to neutralize the effects of whatever chaos may be happening in the world. Color can also have a major impact on people's psychological well-being, productivity, performance, self-esteem, and physical health. These are all good reasons to create environments that foster harmony through the effective use of color.

Most people can remember positive and negative experiences involving color. If you can't easily recall such experiences, I invite you to conduct some experiments by becoming more aware of the colors you choose for clothing or home furnishings. Use this awareness to help you determine which colors affect you with positive energy, which colors have little or no effect on you, and which colors tend to dampen or decrease your energy.

Perhaps you have walked into someone's home and felt strongly affected by its colors. You may have experienced a feeling that was either positive or negative, but either way, colors do induce definite reactions. Dark colors may create feelings of being closed in, cut off, crowded, subdued, or restricted. Could this be one of the reasons why clothing that is black—the darkest of all colors—seems to make people appear smaller in physical form?

Of course, these qualities of dark colors do not mean that you must restrict your selection to all light colors. However, it may be wise to avoid using too many dark colors together in a room. If you do prefer dark colors, just remember to balance them with lighter hues.

Some years ago when I moved into an apartment, the solid beige draperies had to be sent out to the cleaners. In order to retain privacy at the sliding glass door that was usually protected by the drapes, I hung a piece of print fabric that contained the colors yellow, green, and blue. I was pleasantly surprised to see the profound effect of that cheery fabric on everyone who entered the living room through that door. When the original draperies came back from the cleaners, it was hard to put them back up. Unfortunately, since I was renting the apartment, it was not up to me.

Light colors are the energy-giving colors. One of the ways you can draw energy to your nervous system is by surrounding yourself with lighter colors, such as pastels. As a style note, the use of lighter colors has become increasingly common in interior decorating.

Colors can help you express yourself. Homes and workplaces alike can reflect your own individual personality, which is comprised of many traits like those described in the previous chapter. Creating an environment that fully expresses your true nature can be challenging. However, once you choose to consciously develop and express your individuality, it will be easier for you to make choices that support your uniqueness in more effective ways.

The information about color provided below can serve as a source of guidance to help you select colors for your home or work space.

> **Red** – Red is a color that fits well where there is a lot of physical activity. It is a color of excitement and abundant spirit. Red should be used in areas that have more movement happening in them. Limit its use in areas that are used for concentration and relaxation.

> **Orange** – Orange brings a feeling of warmth. It can be used in rooms where fellowship and socialization are the main focus. Orange is a good color when used as a highlight. If it is used excessively, orange will feel overbearing.

> **Yellow** – Yellow provides stimulation to the intellect. It should be used in areas where creative or mental activities are pursued. The color yellow encourages informality, playfulness, and creativity. It radiates optimism and joyfulness.

> **Green** – Green encourages rest and relaxation in a room. It also calms and soothes the nervous system, and it calms the mind. Green helps to provide a feeling of energy and vitality, and it promotes a sense of natural growth and abundance.

> **Blue** – Blue offers many of the same qualities as the color green. It contributes tranquility and peacefulness to its surroundings. Blue is a good color for areas intended for relaxation and rest, and it can be used in rooms that are small in order to give a feeling of spaciousness. However, be sure to use the color blue with care, because too much of it will induce the opposite effect.

> **Purple or Indigo** – A person who is sensitive may be particularly inclined to use the color purple, because it produces feelings of self-assurance. Purple also has a regal sense about it, and it has connotations of a spiritual nature (thus it is sometimes considered a "New Age" color).

> Purple or indigo is a color that must be used sparingly, though it may be useful in rooms where family discussions take place. Too much indigo, however, can lead to separation or withdrawal from others. It's a matter of just enough, but not too much, to create the effect you want.

Violet – Violet brings inspiration for the mind, where dreams and visions abound. It may be useful in rooms where a lot of self-expression and creative imagination require support. Violet is also a good choice in spaces where children play, and it is equally good in rooms used for meditation, reflection, and introspection. As a precaution, too much violet may tend to keep people in a fantasy world, out of touch with reality.

The seven colors described above represent the primary color spectrum, and all other colors fall somewhere within this range of color. For example, the color mauve is a combination of pink and purple. It represents calmness or relaxation. Green and blue together will produce turquoise or aqua. When you use a combination of colors in a room, one color will be dominant over the other colors. The dominant color will play the most significant role in your response to the space.

When you let colors support you in your surroundings, you may begin to notice positive changes in your life. Color can help your life to blossom! Without color, it would seem as though the world was colored with a gray crayon, and you know how that would look: dark and gloomy.

Exploring the theory of color can also be a catalyst to self-discovery. Sometimes color preferences are based on style trends, or on what is "pretty." Yet it is important to be aware of the inherent natural harmony and balance that exists in your environment, and this includes consideration of the element of color.

Everything can contribute to—or detract from—this natural order and flow. If you add harmonious, balanced colors, and lighting to your decorating plan, it can contribute positive and far-reaching effects.

LIGHTING YOUR ENVIRONMENT

Lighting is usually the last budget consideration in interior decorating projects. However, lighting can play a big part in your design, in terms of its psychological and visual effects. Be sure to give lighting ample attention when you work with a space.

Colors will look different in sunlight than under artificial light. When selecting colors, it is important to be consistent and use the same kind of light source to make your decisions. When making color choices, filtered light is preferable to direct sunlight, because direct sunlight will provide too much glare and tend to wash out a color's true vibrancy.

Whether your room uses natural light, artificial light, or a combination of the two, good lighting can alter or enhance existing colors. Since most spaces include a variety of lighting styles, be sure to view your color selections in whatever form(s) of lighting your room will actually use.

I like to encourage people to consider full-spectrum lighting for their home or office spaces. Full-spectrum bulbs cost a little more than ordinary light bulbs, but the benefits you derive from these kinds of lights are well worth the cost. As the name implies, full-spectrum bulbs contain the full spectrum of color, so they closely emulate natural outdoor light. Ultimately, the lighting that you choose will work hand-in-hand with color, and together these elements will be two of your most valuable tools in decorating.

Chapter Five
Decorating Children's Rooms – Essential Elements of Design for Children

Children, like adults, need a place they can call their own. No matter how large or small, it must be a place that reflects the child's individuality. What better way to make this happen than to consider some of the personality traits discussed earlier in this book?

If a child has **High Physical Insulation**, this will indicate some specific needs. First, you might like to choose strong, vivid colors for this child's room. No pastels, please! Solid pieces of furniture would be best, such as those made of wood and coarsely woven fabrics. If children have **Low Physical Insulation**, they will probably prefer colors in lighter tones, and softly textured fabrics would be a better choice for them.

Although this trait was not specifically mentioned in Chapter Three's overview of 12 basic personality traits, you might want to pay attention to a roundness of the ears, which indicates an **Appreciation for Music**. For children with this physiological characteristic, I encourage parents to be sure to include a stereo (or even a radio) in the child's room—anything that produces music.

Another structural trait not mentioned previously is a high forehead, which shows a **High Mental Ceiling**. Children with this personality trait need a place to read, listen to music, or explore a hobby. Quality mental stimulation from books and games would be particularly satisfying for these children.

If a child is **Aesthetic**, she may be more sensitive to what is going on around her. Such a child could be well supported with lovely colors, soothing sounds, and beautiful objects that have personal meaning.

The **Dramatic** child will love to play dress-up. He or she should have a place to build a costume wardrobe that may consist of flowing robes, jewelry, bandannas, or helmets for knights!

All children have special needs during their formative years, and these early years can have a tremendous influence on their entire lives. Help them by creating a supportive environment that can help them discover the power and beauty of their own experience.

Chapter Six

Decorating with Antiques – For Those with the Trait of Backward Balance

Have you ever felt a heavy, overwhelming feeling upon entering a room containing several large pieces of antique furniture? Often this feeling prevails because the room lacks complementary or neutral colors. Colors can help to soften wood tones. Also, when elements of color or texture are added, a greater sense of balance can be projected throughout the room. Heavy or dark can blend with light, soft with hard, and coarse with smooth.

Antique furniture is often medium to dark brown in color. Although wood generally exudes a feeling of warmth, additional color can provide more visual and psychological balance in the space where such furniture exists. When using wood in any area of the home, remember to examine the overall effect.

Does the room need to be softened with splashes of color in the wallpaper or in the accessories? Antiques can be mixed with other styles and periods of furniture if you introduce complementary colors to help unify the different elements into one cohesive design.

Another tip is to avoid grouping all your wood pieces in one area, especially if you are using large pieces of furniture. Wood can easily dominate a room, so take care in how you place these pieces throughout the space.

Once I worked with a client who purchased a large antique chest for her bedroom. She was concerned that the chest would overwhelm the room and take away the soft effect she had created. I suggested that she cover the top of the chest with a piece of light pink marble. As a result, the chest looked less imposing, and the lovely pink marble retained the soft feeling of the woman's bedroom. She was very pleased with the results.

This story is only one of many examples of how you can use color, texture, and other elements of design to successfully integrate the use of antique furniture into your home decor.

Chapter Seven
Planning Your Decorating Project
Originality and individualism are key ingredients.

A PERSONAL PROFILE

You can begin preparing for your decorating project by answering the questions in this chapter to create your own personal profile. Be as specific as you can when you answer the questions. Your answers will provide valuable clues for expressing your individuality in your home or work environment.

COLOR ME PERFECT

What colors do you like best? What colors make you feel good when you are surrounded by them?

Write down all the colors you especially like. These colors will create the palette of choices for your project. Once you've completed your list of colors, select three colors to form the basic color scheme. Make sure the colors you choose have some contrast between them, such as light, medium, and dark.

You might want to buy a color sample guide from your local paint store to help you brainstorm ideas. Another suggestion would be to visit your local art supply store and look at the various poster boards available, since they come in a broad range of colors. In addition, you could browse through pictorial magazines and cut samples of colors from the pictures you like, thus making your own swatches.

If you live with other people, they can let you know color preferences for their own special rooms. For a house theme, you can consider everyone's favorites and brainstorm together to choose three basic colors for the overall house design. Three colors are enough to provide the foundation for your color scheme.

For walls, I recommend that you use neutral colors if you like a feeling of spaciousness with plenty of light. If you have large rooms, you can go a little darker than neutral. With neutral backgrounds, you will be able to expand your use of colors in the room and change them more often, since many different colors blend well with a neutral base. In general, if you prefer dark colors, try using them for draperies, furniture pieces, rugs, and accessories, instead of wall paint.

Sometimes couples can accommodate both people's color choices by having one person select all the lighter colors, while the other chooses the darker ones. Remember that any color is best showcased by contrasting it with other colors. Since colors don't exist in a vacuum, be sure to pay attention to all the ways your color choices interact.

OH, TO BE CLOSE TO YOU!

Do you like a feeling of open space, or do you like a more intimate environment? If you like a feeling of spaciousness, stay with neutral tones for your background colors. Dark colors tend to make a space feel smaller. Personally, I like both of these ingredients in my home.

For a spacious effect, I use my favorite light colors. To create a more intimate feeling, I use dark-colored accessories to maintain a nice balance in my rooms. Textured fabrics and furnishings can also enhance a sense of intimacy.

I'D RATHER BE OUTDOORS!

Do you enjoy the outdoors? If so, your decorating style should include a look that gives you a feeling of being in nature. For instance, you might like a home with a view, with large windows that allow "outside" to become "inside." You might also want to use earth-rich colors that delight your senses, such as taupe, warm grays, or soft greens that remind you of leaves. Dried flower arrangements, large wicker baskets, and stone or tile floors are all great ideas for accenting a nature-lover's space.

A STAR IS BORN!

Do you have a passion for drama, or do you prefer only a touch of showiness? One of my clients gave me a folder with all the magazine pictures she had collected that illustrated rooms she liked. I noticed that every one of them contained a lot of dramatic touches, such as brilliant colors, out-of-the-ordinary accessories, and wood furniture that was built with flair. Most of her favorite rooms also had colorful artwork on the walls and interesting art objects on the tabletops and cabinets.

Obviously, this client had a taste for the dramatic. Almost everything she liked had a quality that said, "Look at me!" For people with the **Dramatic** trait, decorating can be a fun and deeply satisfying way of expressing themselves.

For those of you who prefer only a bit of drama, smaller attention-getters may do the trick. Colorful pillows on a sofa, unusual window treatments, and one-of-a-kind accessories can provide showiness on a lesser scale. Such dramatic touches are like icing on a cake. They add star quality to a room.

YOU CAN HAVE IT ALL!

Do you prefer quality over quantity? Some people like to purchase many items all at once, and they feel great after doing so. Others would rather buy a few expensive items and then decorate around these items, adding additional items of similar high quality as money allows.

If you go for quality over quantity, you probably have an appreciation for well-made or custom-made items. If you seek out expensive furniture and quality paints, you may have to wait to purchase other items. However, if you value quality, you would rather wait than get something that does not measure up to your high standards. Whatever you do in your decorating plan will reflect the fact that your first consideration is *quality*.

On the other hand, if quantity is more important to you, then you might enjoy doing more for less, because you believe you can get what you want without spending a lot of money. If this sounds more like your style, you may have to do some shopping around to find everything on your list.

For most people, quantity and quality will *both* need to be considered in their decorating plans. As always, balance between elements—including a balance between quantity and quality—is the essential key to success.

If you are working with several personalities (and therefore, many different personality traits) for a decorating project, you will need to allow each person to express his or her individual preferences. To do this, choose one or two main personality traits that relate to each person.

Next, gather information about the basic styles that relate to the specific traits you have identified for you and the other people who share your space. Then use these facts to focus on the most important decorating elements that can support each of the personality traits involved.

For example, Bob has **High Physical Insulation**, and Mary has **Low Physical Insulation**. Their overall decorating plan must accommodate these opposing styles. Bob loves the outdoors, coarse textures, and strong colors. Mary is very sensitive, and she likes soft pastels and light, airy environments. Her taste tends toward the refined.

With a little compromise, Mary and Bob can both get their needs met. For instance, their living room could have pastel-colored walls and sturdy furniture made of dark woods. They could use coarsely textured fabrics in the draperies and pillows, and accessories could be understated and of fine quality.

In addition, a high-quality lighting system could be installed with full-spectrum bulbs that would bring out the various colors in their decorating scheme, and large windows could provide ample views of the outdoors. A lush, oversized plant might also be an excellent choice for their living room. Pictures with vivid colors could bring life to the walls. Finally, Bob and Mary could choose one large focal point, such as an elegant armoire or a built-in entertainment system, to help keep things organized and at the same time beautiful.

As you can see from this example, when both traits are taken into consideration, it provides a visual presentation that is a combination of both. In the case of Mary and Bob, a harmonious effect was achieved through the use of coarse textures, strong colors as well as light colors, and touches of refinement. Hopefully, some of these ideas will inspire you and give you a sense of direction as you implement your own decorating plan.

Chapter Eight
Decorating Your Life – Creative Self-Expression
and the Path of Self-Discovery

Creativity can play a vital role in every area of life. By decorating your space with awareness, you can bring more creativity to the core of your existence, adding a sense of playfulness and spiritual energy to your surroundings.

The more you learn about your individuality and uniqueness, the easier it will be to live a life filled with abundance and prosperity. Many people limit prosperity and abundance to material possessions, but the creative spirit within knows that when you tap into it, you can enhance and elevate all areas of life in *unlimited* ways.

Creativity contains a magical ball that radiates an endless supply of positive energy to shape and influence every aspect of your life. You can nourish this creativity with projects that call for original ideas to be transformed into three-dimensional environments that support your work and leisure activities.

When you choose to develop ideas that come from within, you are truly using the personality trait of originality that sets you apart from others. The more this trait is translated into action, the more you can create true wealth—that which arises from your own being. The wealth that comes from discovering and expressing your true self can then add more power and strength to your persona.

Let your decorating projects be lessons in creativity as well as self-exploration. New discoveries about yourself and your environment will increase your level of awareness. A higher level of awareness, in turn, can help you design home and work spaces that will bring more harmony, joy, and fun to your life.

As you continue to explore Personology and its application to interior design, I hope these tools will help you discover more of your potential as a human being. May you celebrate your style and have a good time decorating according to your traits!

Chapter Nine

A Tour of Rooms – Examples of Decorating for Specific Personality Traits

All of the rooms included in this "tour" will illustrate the elements of various personality traits. You will notice that one or two traits tend to dominate each room. **High Physical Insulation** and **Low Physical Insulation** are two of the most important traits. These two traits will usually take precedence over other traits when you apply them to decorating. However, important clues can still be drawn from additional traits.

You can use the examples of these rooms as guides to help you choose decorating styles that express your personal uniqueness. Of course, some of the decorating schemes will appeal to you more than others. If you pay special attention to the rooms you like best, you can discern which elements of design make the most difference to you.

Figure 1
Trait: Idealizing
Characteristic: Low placement of the ears

For this trait, there is a relatively large percentage of the head above the ear compared to most people. The ear might even be as low as the nose opening. Another way to look at this would be to see the ear as sitting close to the collar line. This indicates the trait of idealizing.

Idealizing is one of my own personality traits, and it stimulates a lot of fun for me and my personal decorating projects. Idealizing provides an abundance of creativity. If you share this trait, you may enjoy more lighthearted approach in your decorating scheme, with styles that include shabby chic and a romantic look.

Soft floral prints, checks, stripes, French antiques, and jewel tones exemplify the wide range of choices that the support someone with the trait of idealizing. Lampshades with beads can also be fun, and you could add a touch of whimsy with accessories to create your own eclectic decor. In addition, those with this trait might be happier with furniture and decorating accents not seen anywhere else.

This children's room is a typical example of the idealizing trait. With light colors, colorful accessories accompanied by an overall simple furniture arrangement. Children blossom in this environment.

Figure 2
Trait: Dramatic
Characteristic: High sweeping eyebrows

With this trait, you will require dramatic touches to reflect flair for flamboyance. This person is attracted to any underlying theme that says, "Look at me, this is who I am!" This room with the yellow chair grabs your attention. Having unique items and using different textures and patterns that can stimulate your visual attention.

Trait: Practical
Characteristic: Ears that are positioned higher on the head

This person is more down to earth, less of a romantic, and less wrapped up in a principle or a cause. He or she is more willing to take whatever comes with the territory. If you have the practical trait, the decorating plan for you could well include some items of furniture from the past, or so-called "traditional" items. You may enjoy purchasing antiques for your home, such as a potbelly stove for the kitchen. Family heirlooms can also add to your decorative plan.

Medium to dark colors may have special significance for you and you might like to mix printed fabrics with familiar items you have kept through the years. Rich colors with vibrant patterns may intrigue you and solid, sturdy wood furniture can offer balance.

Figure 3
Trait: High Physical Insulation
Characteristics:
1) **Medium textured skin and hair.**
2) **Coarse skin and hair**

This trait exemplifies a love outdoors in a preference for larger amounts of food than most people want.

What do these preferences mean when you are assessing needs for decorating? No doubt you will be drawn to textured fabrics and vibrant colors. No pastels for you! Furniture that is massive can work well for you, so forget about anything that falls in the category of dainty.

Dark, rich woods, such as mahogany and rosewood, can make a strong statement for you. A few pieces of sculpted furniture can add interest. Above all, furniture should be sturdy and comfortable.

Trait: Aesthetic
Characteristics: Flat, straight eyebrows

If you reflect this straight, you may have a strong need to make your decorating project an extremely creative one. It may be especially meaningful for you to listen to your favorite music while arranging your furniture. Dining by candlelight could be another source of enjoyment for you. Surrounding yourself with harmony is of prime importance. For those who possess the aesthetic trait, it will be essential for you to express your favorite kind of art as a feature ingredient in your decorating. Color is also essential for you, because these represent soothing colors for you.

Of course, each of these components must come together harmoniously in whatever space you are decorating.

Figure 4
Trait: Forward Balance
Characteristic: Position of the ear relative to the front or the back of the head

If you have this trait of forward balance, new and trendy ideas will probably be fun for you. An unusual decor may be especially pleasing to you, and you may enjoy a decorating plan that brings you special attention.

Start with bright colors for the background-colors that inspire you and excite you. You may want a home that you can show off to guess on a tour, eliciting "oohs" and "aahs" as they proceed through the various rooms.

Select accessories that are unique, which serve as conversation pieces. While it is important to have one item in each room as the armoire or a built-in entertainment system to help keep things organized and at the same time beautiful. As you can see from this example, when both traits are taken into consideration, it provides a visual presentation that is a combination of both traits.

Trait: Adventurousness
Characteristics: High prominent cheekbones

What do the faces of American Indians, Mongols, and Vikings, often have in common? They all have high prominent cheekbones, which are characteristic of the adventurousness trait.

If you have this trait, your biggest adventure in life will be your own self-unfoldment. Decorating for you may include a wonderful potpourri of styles, colors, and motifs. Anything goes because you are open to all kinds of ideas.

A mixture of things—such as different periods of furniture—will be par for the course.

It's not likely that you will be satisfied with common trend, because that would only limit the abundance of ideas you already have brewing in your own mind.

People with the trait of adventurousness may want to make changes in their decorating scheme quite often. If you are this kind of person, you might want to change colors, add another accessory, or change the furniture arrangement more often than most. It may help you to work with neutral colors, because they can provide you with a background for frequent color changes in your accent furniture or accessory objects. In addition, pictures or mementos from your travels can also add spice to your decorating theme.

Figure 5
Trait: Practical
Characteristic: High placement of the ears that are positioned higher on the head

This person is more down to earth, less of a romantic, and less wrapped up in a principle or a cause. He or she is more willing to take whatever comes with the territory. If you have the practical trait, the decorating plan for you could well include some items of furniture from the past, or so-called "traditional" items. You may enjoy purchases antiques for your home, such as a potbelly stove for the kitchen. Family heirlooms can also add to your decorative plan.

Medium to dark colors may have special significance for you and you might like to mix printed fabrics with familiar items you have kept through the years. Rich colors with vibrant patterns may intrigue you and solid, sturdy wood furniture can offer balance.

Trait: High Physical Insulation
Characteristic: Course Skin and Hair

People with low physical insulation: pastel or neutral colors would be good color choices. Rough fabrics will not appeal to you as much as finely textured ones, such as silk, satin, and organdy. In addition, it will be essential for you to let your feeling guide you towards colors, comfort, and styles that support your heightened level of sensitivity.

Figure 6
Trait: Dramatic
Characteristic: High sweeping, arched eyebrows

This room is a good example of a combination of traits: Dramatic and Imagination. According to Personology, high sweeping, arched eyebrows represent the dramatic trait. If you possess this trait, you may have a true gift for make believe. You can get into the spirit of a situation. Most likely, you may also find it easy to fit into any role.

The dramatic person loves to make sweeping entrances and exits. Drama and spirit enliven everything they do. Decorating with this trait requires dramatic touches to reflect the personal flair for flamboyance. Perhaps you have visited a home project that has this dramatic flair through the use of furniture or other objects that were entirely different from anything you had ever seen.

Trait: Imaginativeness
Characteristic: Prominent frontal eminences

For you, what makes a room come alive in your imagination? If you possess this trait, you may find it easy to visualize your decorating project entirely in your head. With this gift of imagination, your capacity to come up with great ideas will be limitless. You are probably the kind of person who can have fun with innovative ideas that may not be found in most magazines or decorating books.

Accessories may be a main focus for you, because they can play in important role in pulling a project together.

For you, what makes the room come alive in your imagination? If you possess this trait (imaginativeness), you may find it easy to visualize your decorating project entirely in your head. With this gift of imagination, your capacity to come up with great ideas will be limitless. You are probably the kind of person who can have fun with innovative ideas that may not be found in most magazines or decorating books. Accessories may be a focus for you, because they can play in important role in pulling a project together. For you, accessories will be like spice in food. You may be attracted to unusual items, such as colorful object, conversational pieces, or decorative accents that evoke strong responses because of their uniqueness.

Creatively bound books, artwork from specific cultures, or vases with different textures may appeal to you. Area rugs that display pattern and colors you love can bring excitement to your space. A tip for someone with this trait is to have pictures in a scrapbook that show furnishings and accessories you like just to stimulate your own imagination. Once you have photographic examples, you can use them to help you visualize the kind of space that would most suit you personally. If you have this trait, be sure to take plenty of time to enjoy the process of decorating creatively. Let your imagination flow!

Figure 7
Trait: Dramatic
Characteristic: High sweeping arched eyebrows

This room is a reflection of the dramatic trait. Look at the amazing contrast of light and dark colors together. The white with rich dark wood tones resulting in a rich elegant space that catches your attention. Decorating with this trait requires dramatic touches to reflect the personal flair for splendor.

Chapter Ten
Resources - The Personology Institute, Books, and Interior Design Support

THE PERSONOLOGY INSTITUTE

The Personology Institute is an educational corporation. It is dedicated to the development of Personology educational programs. These programs aim to advance the positive use of natural behavior patterns. Educational training is available for individuals, as well as for business and industry.

Personology is the study of people through the relationship between human structure and behavior. Statistical research and validation work in the field of Personology has identified a close correlation between more than 60 physiological patterns and natural behavioral tendencies. In general, Personology research concludes the following: "Structure indicates natural function, but choice and free will can supersede structure."

Numerous counselors and teachers of Personology in the United States, Canada, and Europe have been trained and certified by the Personology Institute. Personology can be utilized in practical ways by individuals in the following areas:

1) Career guidance and choices;
2) Improved self-understanding and acceptance;
3) Relationships (personal and business);
4) Teaching (better understanding of students' learning styles);
5) Sales seminars (better understanding of clients);
6) Management training seminars.

CONTACT INFORMATION FOR THE PERSONOLOGY INSTITUTE

International Institute
of Personology
507 Capitola Avenue
Capitola, CA 95010-2759
(831) 476-1632

39

Personology Books

Whiteside, Robert. *Face Language*. A guide to meeting the right person.

Whiteside, Robert. *Face Language III*. A guide on how to deal best with important people in your life.

Interior Design Support

Verilux Lighting

www.verilux.com

Room & Board Collection

Photos reproduce by permission: no duplication or reproduction of these photos allowed without the express written permission.

4600 Olson Memorial Highway

Minneapolis, MN 55422

www.roomandboard.com

CPSIA information can be obtained
at www.ICGtesting.com
Printed in the USA
BVRC091303180322
631870BV00002B/3